PESTICIDES

BY
MIGNONNE GUNASEKARA

Cavendish Square
New York

Published in 2023 by Cavendish Square Publishing, LLC
29 East 21st Street
New York, NY 10010

© 2021 Booklife Publishing
This edition is published by arrangement with Booklife Publishing

No part of this publication may be reproduced, stored in a retrieval system, or transmitted in any form or by any means—electronic, mechanical, photocopying, recording, or otherwise—without the prior permission of the copyright owner. Request for permission should be addressed to Permissions, Cavendish Square Publishing, 29 East 21st Street, New York, NY 10010. Tel (877) 980-4450; fax (877) 980-4454.

Website: cavendishsq.com

This publication represents the opinions and views of the author based on his or her personal experience, knowledge, and research. The information in this book serves as a general guide only. The author and publisher have used their best efforts in preparing this book and disclaim liability rising directly or indirectly from the use and application of this book.

All websites were available and accurate when this book was sent to press.

Edited by: William Anthony

Designed by: Danielle Rippengill

Cataloging-in-Publication Data

Names: Gunasekara, Mignonne.
Title: Pesticides / Mignonne Gunasekara.
Description: New York : Cavendish Square, 2023. | Series: People poisons | Includes glossary and index.
Identifiers: ISBN 9781502663726 (pbk.) | ISBN 9781502663740 (library bound) | ISBN 9781502663733 (6 pack) | ISBN 9781502663757 (ebook)
Subjects: LCSH: Pesticides--Health aspects--Juvenile literature. | Pesticides--Environmental aspects--Juvenile literature. | Pesticides--Toxicology--Juvenile literature.
Classification: LCC RA1270.P4 G858 2023 | DDC 363.738'498--dc23

Some of the images in this book illustrate individuals who are models. The depictions do not imply actual situations or events.

CPSIA compliance information: Batch #CSCSQ23. For further information contact Cavendish Square Publishing LLC, New York, New York, at 1-877-980-4450.

Printed in the United States of America

Find us on 🅕 📷

Image Credits

All images are courtesy of Shutterstock.com, unless otherwise specified. With thanks to Getty Images, Thinkstock Photo and iStockphoto. Cover: wow.subtropica, Rayyy, sokolovski, Milan M, hedgehog94, encierro. 4 – WildlifeWorld. 5 – Fotokostic. 6 – Aleksandar Cholanchevski. 7 – ADragan. 8 – nechaevkon. 9 – Carlos Aranguiz. 10 – alicja neumiler. 11 – Elena Masiutkina. 12 – grbender. 13 – nelic. 14 – Ewa Studio. 15 – alicja neumiler. 16 – Smileus. 17 – CHAINFOTO24. 18 – Claudia Naerdemann. 19 – Chumash Maxim. 20 – Kenishirotie. 21 – Morakod1977. 22 – Dmitrii Pridannikov. 23 – hedgehog94.

CONTENTS

PAGE 4 What Are Pesticides?

PAGE 6 Pesticides in Action

PAGE 10 Why Use Pesticides?

PAGE 12 The Dangers of Pesticides

PAGE 14 Everyday Pesticides

PAGE 16 Pesticides in Food Chains

PAGE 20 Reducing Residues

PAGE 23 Remember…

PAGE 24 Glossary and Index

Words that look like *this* can be found in the glossary on page 24.

What Are PESTICIDES?

Many insects, such as locusts, are pests.

Pesticides are used to kill or keep away pests. Pests are plants or animals that are harmful. They can damage crops, hurt livestock, and carry diseases.

Pesticides are often used on farms to **protect** crops from being eaten by pests. They can also stop other plants from growing and taking **nutrients** from the crops.

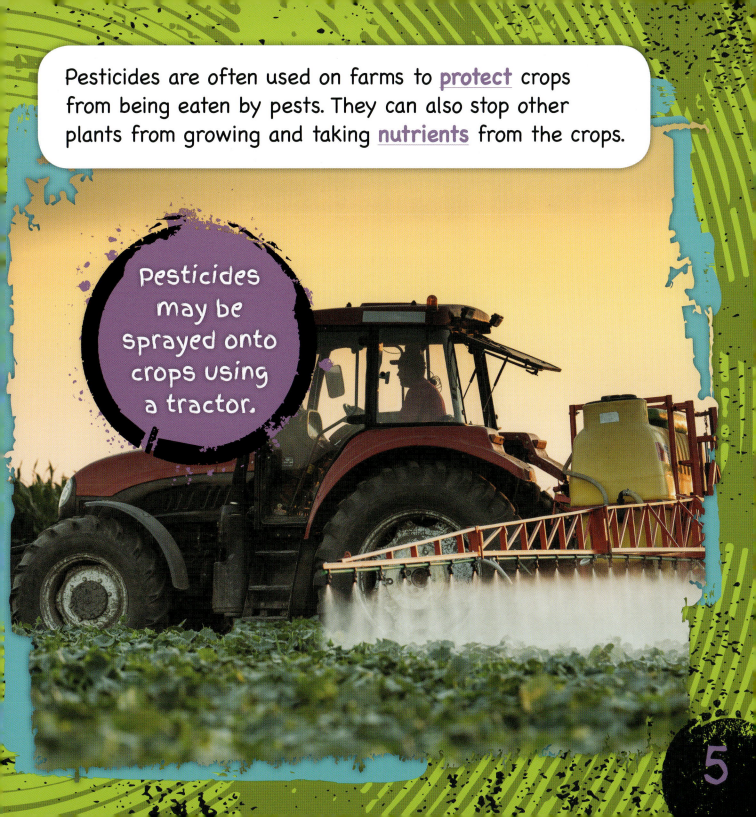

Pesticides may be sprayed onto crops using a tractor.

PESTICIDES in ACTION

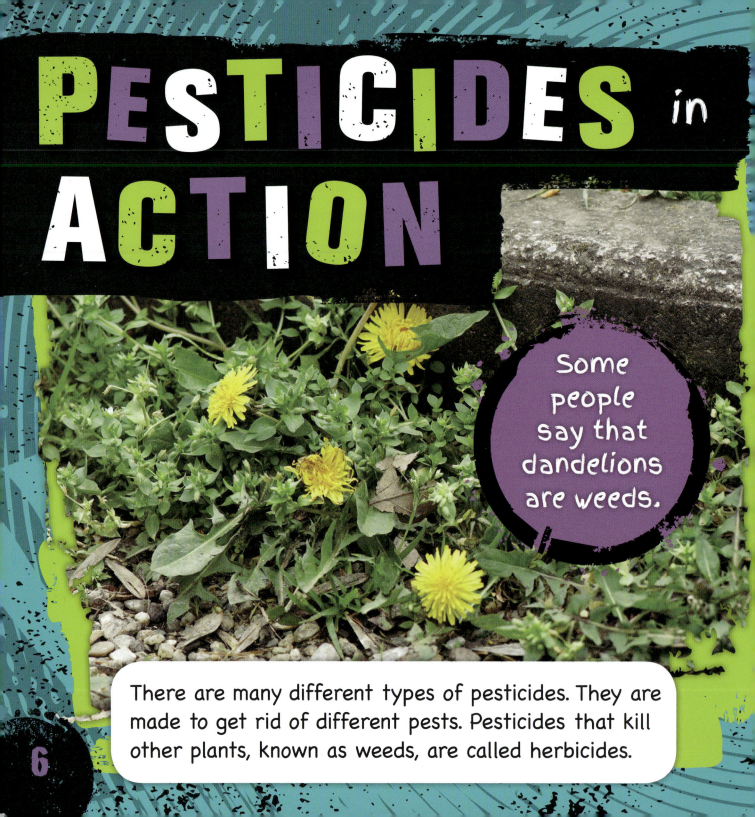

Some people say that dandelions are weeds.

There are many different types of pesticides. They are made to get rid of different pests. Pesticides that kill other plants, known as weeds, are called herbicides.

Fungicides are used to protect crops from harmful fungi that can **rot** crops. Fungi are living things that can look like plants, but can't make their own food like plants can.

This apple has fungus growing on it.

Insecticides kill insects. Some insects eat crops and others can carry diseases. Insecticides can keep insects from passing on diseases to other animals and people.

Mosquitoes are insects that can carry diseases.

Rodenticides kill rodents. Rodents are a group of small animals that includes rats and mice. Rodents may eat growing or stored crops. They can also carry diseases that hurt or kill livestock.

Why Use PESTICIDES?

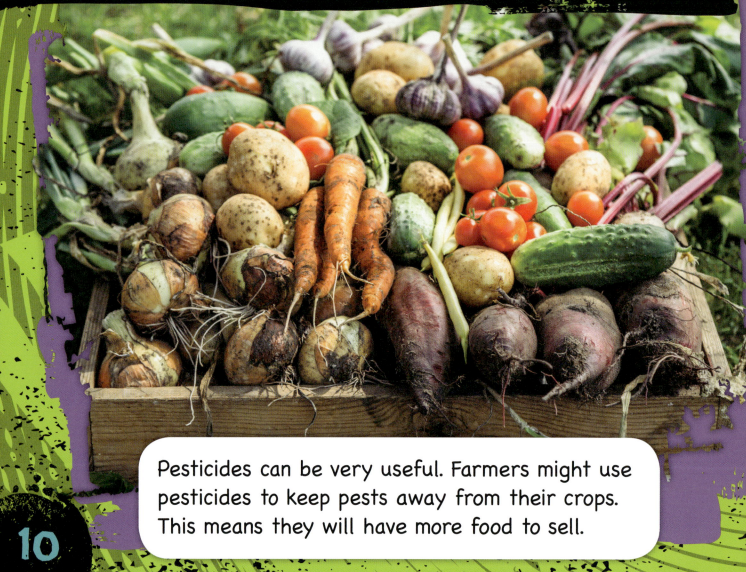

Pesticides can be very useful. Farmers might use pesticides to keep pests away from their crops. This means they will have more food to sell.

Pesticides also stop the spread of disease in crops. This means that farmers will lose fewer crops to disease and will have more food to sell.

These tomatoes have a disease.

The Dangers of PESTICIDES

Pesticides can make people's eyes sore.

Touching or being near pesticides is bad for humans. If a pesticide touches the skin, it may cause a burn. Pesticides can also harm humans if they are breathed in.

People need to wear special clothing to keep pesticides from getting into their bodies whenever they use them.

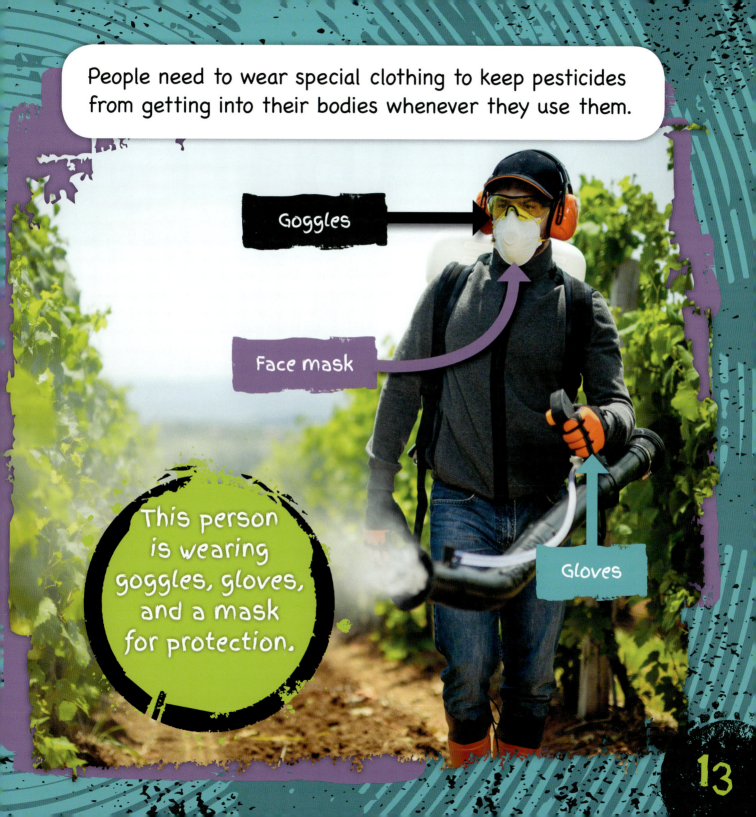

Goggles

Face mask

Gloves

This person is wearing goggles, gloves, and a mask for protection.

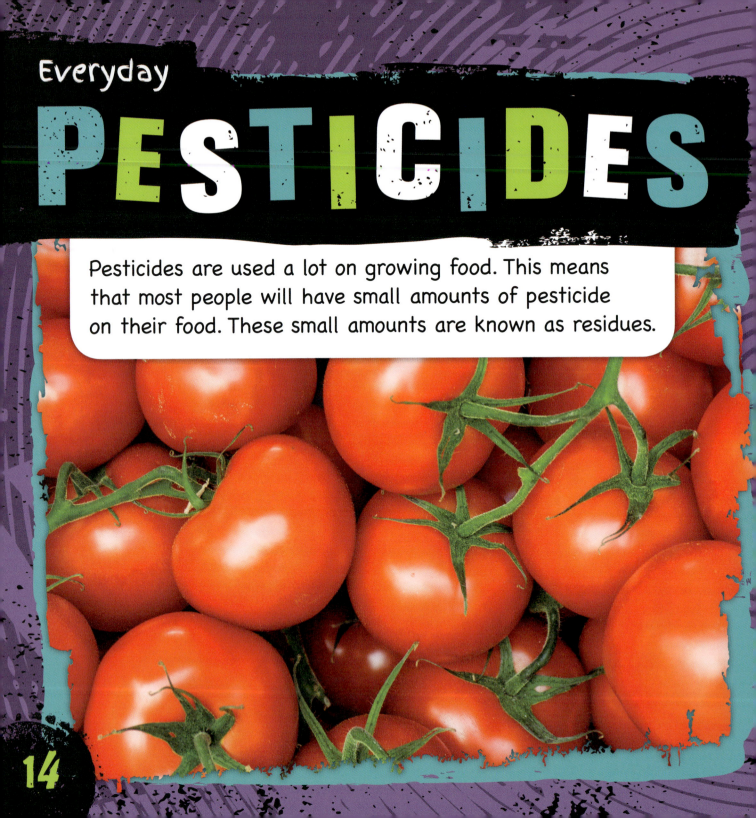

Everyday PESTICIDES

Pesticides are used a lot on growing food. This means that most people will have small amounts of pesticide on their food. These small amounts are known as residues.

Many pesticides break down over time as the crops are picked and moved around. By the time our food is cooked, the amount of pesticide left is so small that it is not thought to be harmful.

PESTICIDES in FOOD CHAINS

Plants are producers.

WHAT IS A FOOD CHAIN?

A food chain shows how **energy** flows through different living things. The first living thing in a food chain is called a producer, because it makes its own food.

Producers are eaten by consumers, and consumers are eaten by other consumers. When a living thing is eaten, its energy and nutrients are passed on.

Consumer

Anything harmful in a food chain also gets passed on.

THE BUILDUP OF PESTICIDES

Pesticides usually get into a food chain when they are used on plants. Animals eat the plants and take in the pesticides, which are then stored in their bodies.

When these animals are eaten by others, the pesticides move up the food chain. This means that animals toward the top of food chains will end up with more pesticides in their food.

Reducing RESIDUES

Buy organic foods, which are usually grown with fewer pesticides.

There are things we can do to reduce the amount of pesticide residues in our food.

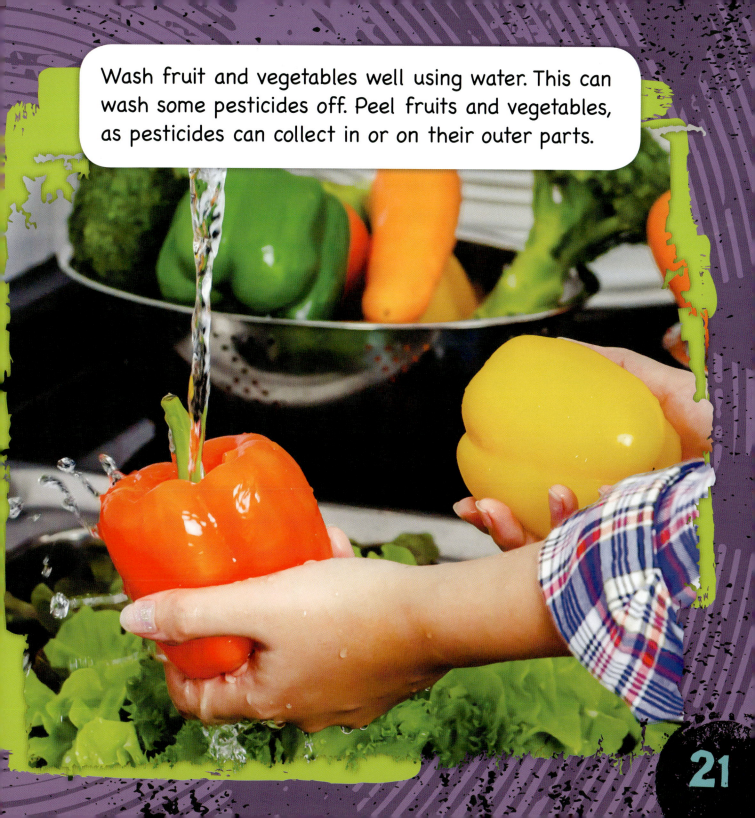
Wash fruit and vegetables well using water. This can wash some pesticides off. Peel fruits and vegetables, as pesticides can collect in or on their outer parts.

Try to cut the fat off the meat and fish you eat, because pesticides can end up stored here. Shop at farmers' markets so you can ask people how the food was grown.

Fat

REMEMBER...

The amount of pesticides normally found on food is not thought to be harmful. We can try to reduce residues, but it is most important to be careful when using or being near pesticides.

GLOSSARY

crops	plants that are grown on a large scale to be eaten or used
diseases	illnesses that cause harm to the health of plants, animals, or people
energy	a type of power that can be used to do something
insects	animals with one or two pairs of wings, six legs, and no backbone
livestock	farm animals that are sold or used to make money
nutrients	natural substances that plants and animals need to grow and stay healthy
protect	to keep something from harm
rot	to break down due to the action of bacteria or fungi
stored	kept for future use

INDEX

crops 4–5, 7–11, 15
diseases 4, 8–9, 11
farmers 10–11, 22
fat 22
food 10–11, 14–16, 19–20, 22–23
food chains 16, 18–19
insects 4, 8
livestock 4, 9
nutrients 5, 17
protective clothing 13
residues 14, 20, 23
skin 12
washing 21
weeds 6